THE MOON.

luna mystic

Moonlight

Shine

Night

Power

Luna

Shine

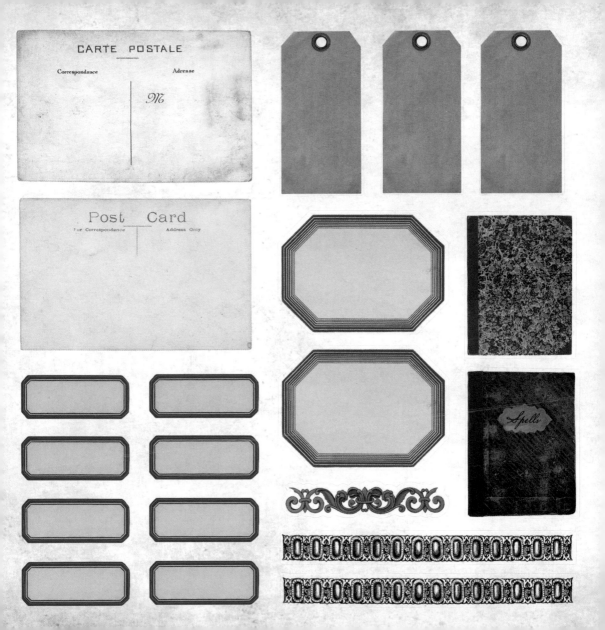

CARTE POSTALE

Correspondance   Adresse

M

Post   Card

For Correspondence   Address Only

Spells

Blessed be

In the midnight hour

If you harm none,
do as you will

Love Potion no. 9

Water of the Moon

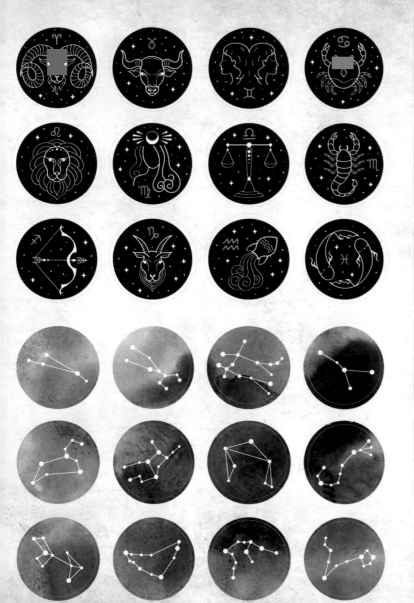

Family Tree

Family

Love

History

Past

Vampire

Bite

Night

Taste

Blood

Thank You

Double, double toil and trouble; Fire burn, and caldron bubble.

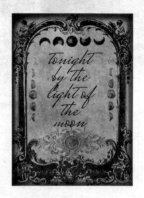

On a full moon night by the dark water the spell is cast. The truth is set free.

Tonight by the light of the moon

She shines bright

Tonight is the night that the spell will be cast. The future is bright for all who believe.

The magic is within her, she cannot fail. The power of the moon guides the way.

believe

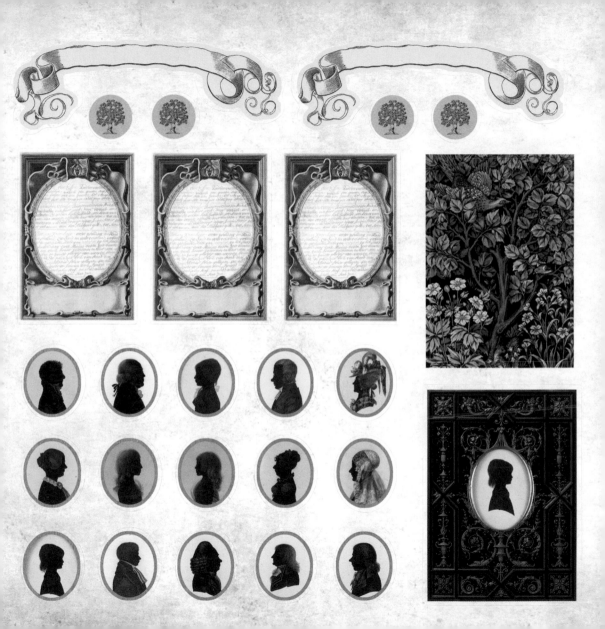

DE FRANCE
of France

PARIS-95

The Secret Garden

PETER HENDERSON & CO

12 Annual
SEED CATALOGUE 1899
SURE TO GROW
LIVINGSTON'S SEED STORE

The Garden   *Grow*

Bloom   *Secret*   *Seeds*

The Witches

Witches

Magic

Wicca

Spells

OLD
DOROTHY CLUTTERBUCK'S
EMPORIUM

The most
spellbinding
additives

WITCH
HAZEL

Hamamelis is a bewitching
way to relieve the most
painful itches caused by
many bug bites.

No cabinet should be
deprived of it!

Wizarding

Spell

Books

Cast

Magic

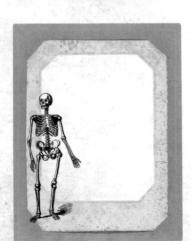

Frog Legs

Rat Tails

Skull Dust

Butterfly Eggs

Wing of Bat

Snail Slime

Moon Beams

Mermaid Tears

Scorpion Sting

Crow Feathers

Serpent Scales

Diamond Dust

Absinthe

Owl Talon

Toad Warts

Dragonfly Wings

Viper Venom

Nightshade

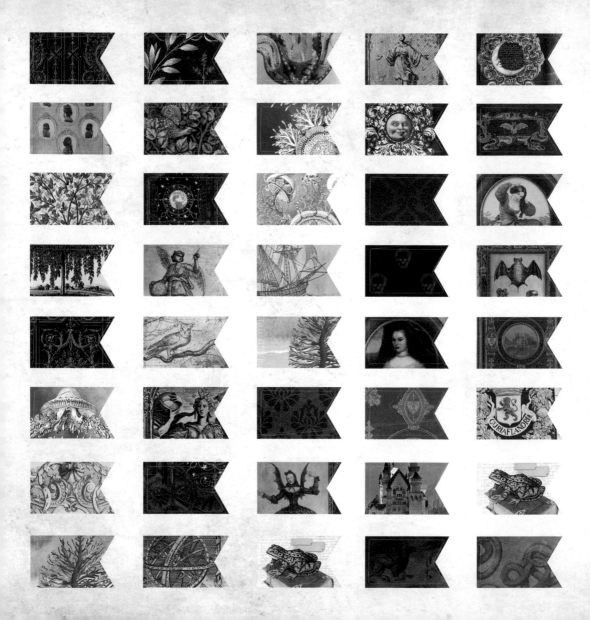

Wat hier leeres oft bril, als den WL niet sienen wil.

Spells

&

Magic

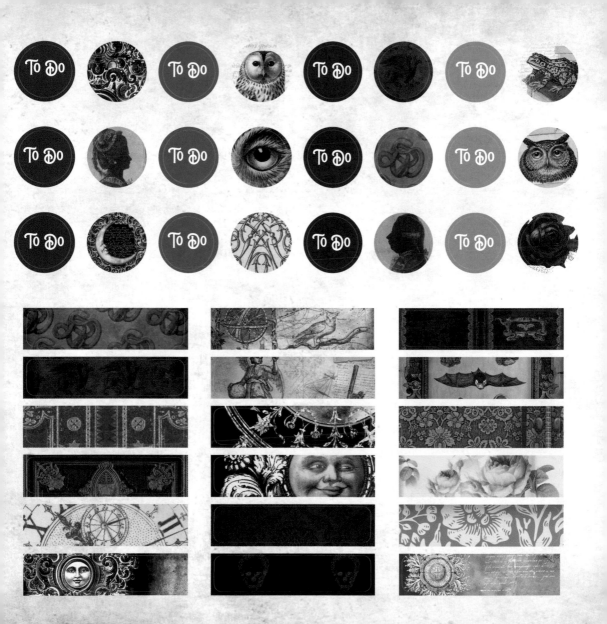

Potion to heal the faint of heart

Potion to mend a broken heart

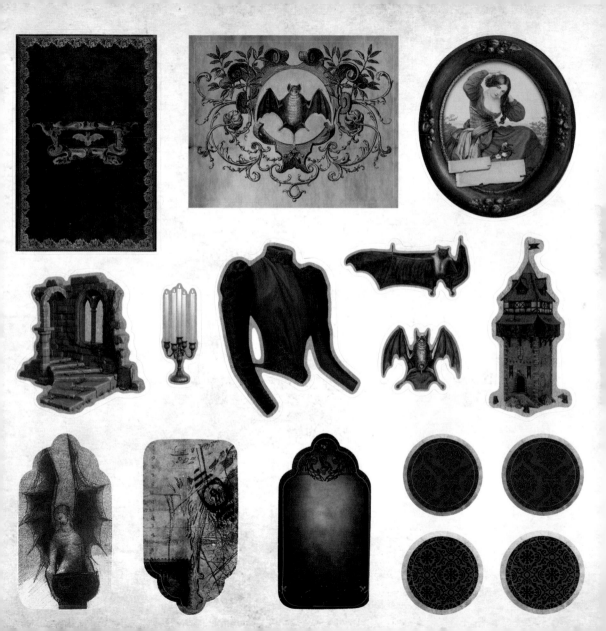